Bond

English
Assessment Papers

5–6 years

Sarah Lindsay

Text © Sarah Lindsay 2007
Original illustrations © Nelson Thornes Ltd 2007

The right of Sarah Lindsay to be identified as author of this work has been asserted by her in accordance with the Copyright, Designs and Patents Act 1988.

All rights reserved. No part of this publication may be reproduced or transmitted in any form or by any means, electronic or mechanical, including photocopy, recording or any information storage and retrieval system, without permission in writing from the publisher or under licence from the Copyright Licensing Agency Limited, of Saffron House, 6–10 Kirby Street, London, EC1N 8TS.

Any person who commits any unauthorised act in relation to this publication may be liable to criminal prosecution and civil claims for damages.

Published in 2007 by:
Nelson Thornes Ltd
Delta Place
27 Bath Road
CHELTENHAM
GL53 7TH
United Kingdom

11/ 10 9 8 7

A catalogue record for this book is available from the British Library

ISBN 978 0 7487 8464 6

Illustrations by Nigel Kitching
Page make-up by GreenGate Publishing Services, Tonbridge, Kent

Printed and bound in Egypt by Sahara Printing Company

Acknowledgements

Extract from *The Runaway Tractor* reproduced from *Complete Book of Farmyard Tales* by permission of Usborne Publishing, 83–85 Saffron Hill, London, EC1N 8RT, UK. www.usborne.com. Copyright © 2004 Usborne Publishing Ltd; Extract from *Then down came the rain* by John Jackman and Hilary Frost first published by Stanley Thornes (Publishers) Ltd reproduced by permission of the authors; Extract from *First Experiences – Moving House* reproduced by permission of Usborne Publishing, 83–85 Saffron Hill, London, EC1N 8RT, UK. www.usborne.com. Copyright © 2002 Usborne Publishing Ltd; "When the Wind Blows" copyright © John Foster 1991 from *Four O'Clock Friday* (Oxford University Press) included by permission of the author; Extract from "Full of the Moon" from *In the Middle of the Trees* by Karla Kuskin copyright © 1959, renewed 1986 by Karla Kuskin. Used by permission of Scott Treimell NY; Extract from "Roger the Dog" by Ted Hughes from *Collected Animal Poems Volume 2 What is the Truth?* by Ted Hughes used by permission of the publishers, Faber and Faber Ltd; Extract from *The Cat in the Hat* by Dr. Seuss, copyright TM and copyright © by Dr. Seuss Enterprises, L.P. 1957, renewed 1985. Used by permission of Random House Children's Books, a division of Random House, Inc.

Before you get started

What is Bond?

This book is part of the Bond Assessment Papers series for English, which provides **thorough and continuous practice of key English skills** from ages five to thirteen. Bond's English resources are ideal preparation for many different kinds of tests and exams – from SATs to 11+ and other secondary school selection exams.

What does this book cover?

It practises comprehension, spelling, grammar, punctuation and vocabulary work appropriate for children of this age. It is fully in line with the National Curriculum for English and the National Literacy Strategy. One of the key features of Bond Assessment Papers is that each one practises **a wide variety of skills and question types** so that children are always challenged to think – and don't get bored repeating the same question type again and again. We think that variety is the key to effective learning. It helps children 'think on their feet' and cope with the unexpected.

The age given on the cover is for guidance only. As the papers are designed to be reasonably challenging for the age group, any one child may naturally find him or herself working above or below the stated age. The important thing is that children are always encouraged by their performance. Working at the right level is the key to this.

What does the book contain?

- **20 papers** – each one contains 15 questions.
- **Scoring devices** – there are score boxes in the margins and a Progress Chart at the back. The chart is a visual and motivating way for children to see how they are doing. Encouraging them to colour in the chart as they go along and to try to beat their last score can be highly effective!
- **Next Steps** – advice on what to do after finishing the papers can be found on the inside back cover.
- **Answers** – located in an easily-removed central pull-out section. If you lose your answers, please email cservices@nelsonthornes.com for another copy.

How can you use this book?

One of the great strengths of Bond Assessment Papers is their flexibility. They can be used at home, school and by tutors to:

- provide regular English practice in **bite-sized chunks**
- **highlight strengths and weaknesses** in the core skills
- identify **individual needs**
- set **homework**
- set **timed formal practice** tests – allow about 25 minutes.

It is best to start at the beginning and work though the papers in order.

What does a score mean and how can it be improved?

If children colour in the Progress Chart at the back, this will give an idea of how they are doing. The Next Steps inside the back cover will help you to decide what to do next to help a child progress. We suggest that it is always valuable to go over any wrong answers with children.

Don't forget the website…!

Visit www.bond11plus.co.uk for lots of advice, information and suggestions on everything to do with Bond, helping children to do their best, and exams.

Paper 1

There Was a Crooked Man

There was a crooked man,
And he walked a crooked mile,
He found a crooked sixpence
Against a crooked stile;
He bought a crooked cat,
Which caught a crooked mouse,
And they all lived together
In a little crooked house.

                                        Anon

Underline the right answers.

1 How far did the crooked man walk?

(a metre, a mile, a short way)

2 Where did the man find the crooked sixpence?

(against a stile, on a gate, by a fence)

Answer these questions.

3 Which word is in most lines of the poem?

_____

4 Which word in the poem rhymes with **mouse**?

_____

Add the missing full stops to these sentences.

5 Harry slipped and cut his knee

6 Jacob ran home quickly

7 Tia played with her dolls

Make three words, each using three of these letters.

Here is an example: b e d

    e   a   b   t   c   d   m

8 __ __ __   9 __ __ __   10 __ __ __   3

Copy the colour word that matches the colour of these things.

    green   white   yellow

11 a swan   _____

12 grass   _____

13 a banana _____

Write a title to go with each picture.

14

_____

15

_____

Now go to the Progress Chart to record your score!   Total 15

Paper 2

Look at these pictures.

Aimee is showing us how to make a bowl of cereal.

A   **B**   **C**   **D**

Underline the right answers.

1. What does Aimee put on the table with her bowl?

   (cereal, cup, spoon)

2. What does Aimee pour on her cereal?

   (sugar, milk, juice)

Write some **instructions** for making a bowl of cereal.

Write an instruction for each picture. The first one has been done for you.

     A   *First put the bowl, spoon, cereal and milk on the table.*

3. B _____

4. C _____

5. D _____

Write these letters in alphabetical order.

6. d   c   e   ___ ___ ___

7. m   l   k   ___ ___ ___

8. s   u   t   ___ ___ ___

Underline the capital letter and circle the full stop in each sentence.

9 Anil walks to school.

10 Beth plays football.

11 Jake swims every day.

12 Kim feeds her fish.

In each sentence, write what you think the word in **bold** means.

13 The cat **shot** over the fence.

   shot means _____

14 The snow **clung** to the tree.

   clung means _____

15 Ben's clothes were **soaked** after he fell in the pond.

   soaked means _____

Now go to the Progress Chart to record your score!   Total 15

Paper 3

The Runaway Tractor

Ted is driving his tractor pulling a trailer with hay. Poppy and Sam, who live on the farm, hear a funny noise…

They run to the top of the hill. The tractor is racing down the hill, going faster and faster. "It won't stop," shouts Ted.
The trailer comes off. The trailer runs down the hill and crashes into a fence. It tips up and all the hay falls out.
The tractor runs into the pond. The tractor hits the water with a great splash. The engine makes a loud noise, then it stops with a hiss.
Ted climbs down from the tractor. Ted paddles through the water and out of the pond. Poppy and Sam run down the hill.
Ted is very wet. Ted takes off his boots and tips out the water. How can he get the tractor out of the pond?

From *The Complete Book of Farmyard Tales* by Heather Amery

Underline the right answers.

1 Who drives the tractor?

(Poppy, Ted, Sam)

2 What is the trailer carrying?

(hay, sheep, boots)

Answer these questions.

3 What does the trailer crash into?

4 How do you think Ted feels at the end of the story? Why?

Which words rhyme?

Match the rhyming words with a line.

    5 dog   ten

    6 hen   box

    7 cat   log

    8 fox   bat

Write each of these names with a capital letter.

    9 ben _____   **10** meena _____

    11 luke _____   **12** eva _____

Each sentence has a word missing.

Copy the sentence but add a word to help it make sense.

    13 The cat in the sun.

_____

    14 I my teeth every day.

_____

    15 Tom loves to on his bike.

_____

Now go to the Progress Chart to record your score!   Total

Paper 4

The teacher hasn't finished writing these signs.

Add a word from the box to each sign.

1–4 | PE kits   coats   boots   bags

Underline the sentences.

5 Hannah ate all her lunch.   dropped pudding floor

6 sleep in the middle   We jumped over the wall.

7 Ali ran after the dog.   cat climbed tree

Start or finish these words correctly with *f* or *ff*.

8 cli____

9 sni____

10 ___ly   11 pu___   4

Underline the day of the week in each sentence.

12 It is Lily's birthday on Sunday.

13 On Tuesday we are going on holiday.

14 Friday was very busy because my cat had kittens.

15 In May, I have swimming lessons every Saturday.   4

Now go to the Progress Chart to record your score!   Total   15

Paper 5

This is the beginning of the fairy tale *Cinderella*.

Cinderella lived with her two ugly step-sisters. She was made to do all the jobs around the house like scrubbing floors and cooking.
The two ugly sisters wore lovely clothes but all Cinderella was given to wear were rags.
One day an invitation arrived. Everyone in the house was invited to Prince Charming's Ball that evening.
The ugly sisters rushed around getting ready. Cinderella had to help them. She didn't have time to get anything ready for herself. The ugly sisters even gave her jobs to keep her busy while they were at the Ball.
Cinderella felt very unhappy. She cried as she waved goodbye to the ugly sisters.

Underline the right answers.

1 What does Cinderella have to scrub?

(pots, clothes, floors)

2 Who was the invitation from?

(Prince Charming, Princess Charming, King Charming)

Answer these questions.

3 Who helped the ugly sisters get ready?

_____

4 Why do you think Cinderella felt unhappy?

_____

Add the missing full stops.

5–6 The dog chased the cat It ran up the tree

7–8 Harry threw sand in Kyle's face Kyle ran away screaming

Write a rhyming word for each of these words.

9 book _____

10 cat _____

11 bug _____

12 net _____

Choose the best word to fill the gap.

    chasing   chased   chase

13 The puppy _____ the ball.

    sleeping   sleep   slept

14 Sam _____ at Tom's house.

    Them   They   It

15 _____ all loved watching the ice skating.

Now go to the Progress Chart to record your score! Total 15

Paper 6

Kim and Jamie wondered what they could do today.
They decided to write a list of all the things they like to do.
It helped them decide what they could do today!
Here is their list.

> **Things we like to do**
> Build a junk model car.
> Watch television.
> Make some fairy cakes.
> Play pirates on the climbing frame.

Underline the right answer.

1 Which game did they want to play on the climbing frame?

   (fairies, cars, pirates)

Answer the questions.

2 Kim and Jamie thought they could do something in the kitchen. What was it?

   _____

3 Write one thing Kim and Jamie could do inside.

   _____

4 Write one thing Kim and Jamie could only do outside.

   _____

Add *all* and *ell* to make words that match the pictures.

5   b_____   b_____

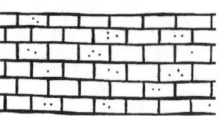 

6   w_____   w_____

7   t_____   t_____

Write the sentences.

Put the words in order.

8 with the puppy. Jay played

_____

9 lovely. The flowers smelt

_____

10 the cake on the floor. Seeta dropped

_____

Label the PE equipment.

11–13 rubber rings   tennis balls   skipping ropes

_____   _____   _____

Write these sentences correctly.

Some capital letters are missing.

14 When i was four i learnt to ride a bike.

_____

15 i love sleeping at alice's house.

_____

Now go to the Progress Chart to record your score!   Total   15

Paper 7

Then down came the rain

Rob and Sue were camping with their parents and some friends. Overnight it rained very hard…

(The next day.)

Rob It is wet. It is very wet in the tents.
Sue It is no fun on holiday in the rain.
Rob We are all wet. The tents are all wet.
Sue Yes, let's go home.

Mum Help us take the tents down.
Dad Help us pack the car.

(All the children look at the car in the mud.)

Dad Oh, no!
Mum Are we stuck?
Dad We are! We are stuck in the mud.
We are very stuck!
All We can help! We will help!

(Dad gets in the car. Mum and all the children push.)

Dad Good! That did it!
All Oh no! Err! Ah! Oo!

(Dad looks out of the car.)

Dad Oh! You are all wet and muddy!
But you did help, you did all help a lot!

(They all think it is funny.)

From *Then down came the rain* by John Jackman and Hilary Frost

Underline the right answers.

1 Why do they decide to go home?

(It is too cold. It is too hot. It is too wet.)

2 Who gets in the car?

(the children, Dad, Mum)

Answer these questions.

3 Where is the car stuck?

_____

4 Why were the children laughing at the end of the story?

_____

Add the missing capital letters and full stops to these sentences.

5 my sister loves chocolate ice cream

_____

6 we are going swimming

_____

7 daniel bought a car magazine

_____

Add *ng* or *nd* to the letters to make a word.

8 lo____ ____

9 se____ ____

10 sou____ ____

11 ga____ ____

Make these sentences more interesting.
Choose a different word for the word in **bold**.

12 I **like** my rabbit.   _____

13 The cake was **nice**.   _____

Sort the letters. Which months are they?

14 r h a M c _____

15 c e D m e e b r _____

Now go to the Progress Chart to record your score!   Total

Paper 8

Thumbelina

One day a magic seed was planted in a pot. In time the seed grew into a flower. When this special flower opened a surprise was found. Inside the flower sat a happy, beautiful girl called Thumbelina. She was like any other girl but she was very small. She was smaller than your thumb!
She slept in a nutshell and used petals as covers. If one drop of water hit her she looked like she had been in a water fight! Thumbelina enjoyed chatting and playing with insects but wondered if she would ever meet someone her own size.

Underline the right answers.

1 Why do you think the girl was called Thumbelina?

(because she was beautiful, because she lived on a thumb, because she was smaller than a thumb)

2 Where did Thumbelina sleep?

(on a petal, in a nutshell, in a bed)

Answer these questions.

3 If Thumbelina was your friend, what would you enjoy doing with her that you cannot do with friends your own size?

_____

_____

4 How do you think Thumbelina felt, being as small as she was?

_____

_____

Look at this picture.

Write four things in the picture that have *sh* or *ch* in them.

5–8 _____   _____

_____   _____

Now write three sentences about the picture.

Remember to use capital letters and full stops.

9–11 _____

_____

_____

_____

Add a word from the box to each gap.

| forgotten | rushed | What | excited |

12 "_____ time is the party?" asked Tom.

13 He was so _____ about going to the Bike Party.

14–15 At last his mum took him to the party but he had _____ out of the house and _____ the present!

Now go to the Progress Chart to record your score!   Total   15

Paper 9

Look at this page from a picture dictionary.
You will find words in alphabetical order in a dictionary.

Underline the right answers.

1 Which word comes before **tea**?
   (table, teacher, ten)

2 Which word comes after **tooth**?

(television, tiger, tractor)

Answer this question.

3 Which letter comes after *t* in the alphabet? _____

Find a short word in each of these words.

Here is an example: stop   *top*

4 shop _____   5 crush _____

6 hill _____   7 clap _____

In each sentence, write what you think each word in **bold** means.

8 James **gulped** down the milk shake.

gulped means _____

9 Hannah felt **nervous** when it was her turn to speak in assembly.

nervous means _____

Look carefully at this piece of writing.

Underline all the capital letters and circle the full stops.

10–12 Nazar was very happy. He had just learnt how to swim. It had been worth practising so hard.

Underline the odd word out.

13 find   kind   send   mind
14 clock   flock   sock   lick
15 coat   load   road   toad

Now go to the Progress Chart to record your score!   Total 15

Paper 10

Moving House

Mr and Mrs Spark, Sophie and Sam are moving house...

The Sparks go to see their new house. The house is being painted before the Sparks move in. Mr Spark makes friends with the people who live next door. Two men from Cosy Carpets arrive to put new carpets down in some of the rooms.

The Sparks pack up their old house. It takes many days for Mr and Mrs Spark to sort out all of their things. Packing is hard work. Sam makes sure that all of his things are packed too. But Sophie would rather play.

The Sparks move. Early in the morning, a big removal truck arrives to take the Sparks' furniture to their new home. Bill, the driver, and Frank and Bess, his helpers, load everything into the big truck. Then they drive it to the new house.

Everyone helps unload the truck. Bill shows Sam and Sophie the inside of the truck. Then they all start to take the things into the new house.

From *Moving House* by Anne Civardi

Underline the right answers.

1 Who did Mr Spark make friends with?

(two men from Cosy Carpets, Bill the driver, the people next door)

2 When did the truck arrive?

(early in the morning, at lunchtime, in the evening)

Answer these questions.

3 What does Bill show Sam and Sophie?

_____

4 What do you think happened when the removal men had gone?

_____

Look at these words. Circle the first letter in each word.
Write the words in the order they come in the alphabet.

    beach   donkey   clock   apple

5–8 _____ _____ _____ _____

Write a *cl* word to match each picture.

9 _____

10 _____

11 _____

12 _____

Some questions will be answered in the children's own words. Answers to these questions are given in *italics*. Any answers that seem to be in line with these should be marked correct.

Paper 1

1 a mile
2 against a stile
3 crooked
4 house
5 Harry slipped and cut his knee.
6 Jacob ran home quickly.
7 Tia played with her dolls.
8–10 *bat, mad, bad, cat*
11 white
12 green
13 yellow
14–15 *Answer showing child's own titles to match the pictures.*

Paper 2

1 spoon
2 milk
3B *Pour the cereal into the bowl.*
4C *Pour the milk onto the cereal/Pour the milk into the bowl.*
5D *Eat the cereal.*
6 c   d   e
7 k   l   m
8 s   t   u
9 Anil walks to school.
10 Beth plays football.
11 Jake swims every day.
12 Kim feeds her fish.
13 *jumped, raced*
14 *stuck to, covered*
15 *wet, dripping*

Paper 3

1 Ted
2 hay
3 The trailer crashes into a fence.
4 *Answer stating how Ted feels at the end of the story and why, e.g. mad because he has to get the tractor out of the pond/is wet from landing in the pond.*

5 dog – log
6 hen – ten
7 cat – bat
8 fox – box
9 Ben
10 Meena
11 Luke
12 Eva
13 The cat *slept/lay* in the sun.
14 I *brush* my teeth every day.
15 Tom loves to *ride/play* on his bike.

Paper 4

1–4 *Answer showing missing signs added to the correct places on the picture.*
5 Hannah ate all her lunch.
6 We jumped over the wall.
7 Ali ran after the dog.
8 cliff
9 sniff
10 fly
11 puff
12 It is Lily's birthday on Sunday.
13 On Tuesday we are going on holiday.
14 Friday was very busy because my cat had kittens.
15 In May, I have swimming lessons every Saturday.

Paper 5

1 floors
2 Prince Charming
3 Cinderella
4 *Answer stating why the child thinks Cinderella is unhappy, e.g. Because she is left out from going to the ball/being treated unfairly/having to help the ugly sisters/having to clean.*
5–6 The dog chased the cat. It ran up the tree.
7–8 Harry threw sand in Kyle's face. Kyle ran away screaming.
9 *look, took, cook*
10 *hat, mat, sat*
11 *rug, hug, mug*

12 *met, set, let*
13 The puppy **chased** the ball.
14 Sam **slept** at Tom's house.
15 **They** all loved watching the ice skating.

Paper 6

1 pirates
2 Kim and Jamie could make some fairy cakes.
3 Watch television, build a junk model car, make some fairy cakes
4 Play pirates on the climbing frame
5 ball
   bell
6 wall
   well
7 tall
   tell
8 Jay played with the puppy.
9 The flowers smelt lovely.
10 Seeta dropped the cake on the floor.
11–13 Answer showing the PE equipment labelled correctly.
14 When **I** was four **I** learnt to ride a bike.
15 **I** love sleeping at **A**lice's house.

Paper 7

1 It is too wet.
2 Dad
3 The car is stuck in the mud.
4 *The children were laughing because they got wet and muddy.*
5 My sister loves chocolate ice cream⊙
6 We are going swimming⊙
7 Daniel bought a car magazine⊙
8 long
9 send
10 sound
11 gang
12 *love, hug, pet*
13 *lovely, tasty*
14 March
15 December

Paper 8

1 because she was smaller than a thumb.
2 in a nutshell
3 Answer stating what they would do with Thumbelina, e.g. *Put her in my pocket and take her out with me, have her sit on my shoulder.*
4 Answer stating what the child thought Thumbelina felt about being so small, e.g. *She felt lonely because there was no one else of her own size.*
5–8 *child/children, bench, shop, fish, chips, ship, chain*
9–11 Answer showing three sentences about the picture with correct use of capital letters and full stops.
12 "**What** time is the party?" asked Tom.
13 He was so **excited** about going to the Bike Party.
14–15 At last his mum took him to the party but he had **rushed** out of the house and **forgotten** the present!

Paper 9

1 table
2 tractor
3 u
4 hop
5 rush, us
6 ill
7 lap
8 *drank quickly*
9 *scared, frightened*
10–12 Nazar was very happy⊙ He had just learnt how to swim⊙ It had been worth practising so hard⊙
13 send
14 lick
15 coat

Paper 10

1 the people next door.
2 early in the morning.
3 Bill shows Sam and Sophie the inside of the truck.

4 *They unpacked, looked around the house, rested.*
5–8 ⓐpple ⓑeach ⓒlock ⓓonkey
9 clip
10 clap
11 clock
12 cliff
13–15 Answer showing child's own names for each picture, with correctly capitalised titles.

Paper 11

1 open wide
2 hide
3 *wiggle them, snap them, scratch, pinch*
4 Where rabbits live
5 What do rabbits eat?
6 Baby rabbits
7–9 *trip, trap, truck, train, try, trick, tray, trail*
10–11 Two sentences written about a 'best friend' with all capital letters and full stops included.
12 drinks
13 flags
14 shops
15 goats

Paper 12

1 6–10 puppies
2 two weeks
3 litter
4 A title *e.g. How puppies become dogs.*
5 sink – drink
6 dress – mess
7 mist – fist
8 match – catch
9 Josie **ran** all the way home.
10 We **packed** our clothes in the suitcase.
11 Leela loved **her** riding lessons.
12 Junior Dictionary
13 A Kangaroo's Home
14 Learning to Swim
15 The Journey

Paper 13

1 6
2 mutter
3 battle
4 Answer stating whether poem would make child go out in wind and why, e.g. *No, because it seems scary outside; Yes, because it would be fun to play when the wind is blowing things around.*
5–7 What is the time?
Where is my PE kit?
Which book do you enjoy?
8 step
9 sting
10 dust
11 What shall I wear?
12 Dean painted a beautiful picture.
13 walked
14 helped
15 called

Paper 14

1–2 Answer showing the labels added correctly to the artwork.
3–4 Answer showing child's own answers correctly labelled.
5 flock
6 flame
7 slug
8 flat or slat
9 slot
10 **Have** you brought your coat?
11 **One** evening Mum let us stay up to watch the fireworks.
12 Meena has collected **so** many blackberries she cannot hold them all!
13 *grabbed*
14 *loves*
15 *stomped, ran*

Paper 15

1 I Hear Thunder
2 *Because it keeps trying to climb up the spout even though the rain keeps knocking it back down.*

3 dry or I
4 rain
5–7 i   a   u
8–9 Daniel is <u>move</u> to a new school.
moving
10–11 The dog loved his morning <u>walked</u>.   walk or walks
12–13 *spout, spin, spill, spoon, spring*
14–15 Answer showing each 'sp' word written in a sentence.

Paper 16

1 Thursday
2 3
3 First Class I saw the cows being milked.
4 They were excited to get their bottles of milk.
5 He said that it was great to visit the farm and that he wanted to go back again.
6 sheet, seat
7 seal, sleep
8 *reading, playing, talking*
9 *washed, looked at*
10 *soaked, fell on, caught*
11 school
12 house
13 laugh
14 <u>I</u> always forget to hand my dinner money in.
15 Today <u>I</u> have to remember my homework.

Paper 17

1 dogs
2 Full of the Moon
3 ease/fleas; head/bread; dog/log; foot/put
4 Roger is an old dog because he sleeps all of the time/doesn't do much.
5–6 Answer showing two sentences about a dog, each with a full stop used correctly.
7 calling
8 walking
9 lifting
10–13 snail, tale, hay, cape
14 <u>Q</u>ueen <u>E</u>lizabeth
15 <u>S</u>ir <u>G</u>areth <u>B</u>igears

Paper 18

1 cloudy
2 windy
3 3
4 Sunday
5–8 my   high   pie   sky
9–10 Answer showing two questions each with a question mark used correctly.
11–12 *ran, went, walked, cycled*
13–15 r   k   v

Paper 19

1 a snake and some beetles
2 Yes
3 *Didgeridoos, because she said it was fun.*
4 blue
5 pink
6 brown
7 What time am I going to the party?
8 The cows munch the grass in the field.
9–12 coat   nose   snow   doze
13 What we eat
14 Inside our bodies
15 What happens when we sleep?

Paper 20

1 wet
2 hat, that, mat or sat
3 The Cat in the Hat wants the children to have fun.
4 The Rat Meets a Cat
5 A Windy Day
6 What Not to Eat
7–8 *How did the dog get on the bus? Where is the dog going? How will the woman get her dog back?*
9–12 *sunny, fun, play, swim, sea*
13 *toy, joy*
14 *flew, chew*
15 *moon, spoon*

Look at these portraits. Give each person a name and a title like Mr, Mrs or Miss.

Remember to use capital letters.

13 _____   14 _____   15 _____

Now go to the Progress Chart to record your score!   Total   15

Paper 11

This rhyme can be done to actions.
As you read it, try to do the actions.

Ten Little Fingers

I have ten little fingers,
And they all belong to me.
I can make them do things,
Would you like to see?
I can shut them up tight,
Or open them all wide.
Put them all together,
Or make them all hide.
I can make them jump high;
I can make them jump low.
I can fold them quietly,
And hold them all just so.

Anon

Underline the right answer.

1 What do the fingers do after they have been shut up tight?

(open wide, jump low, fold quietly)

Answer these questions.

2 Which word in the poem, rhymes with **wide**? _____

3 What else can you do with your fingers?

_____

These headings can be found in a book about rabbits.

Copy each heading. Remember to add the capital letters.

4 where rabbits live _____

5 what do rabbits eat? _____

6 baby rabbits _____

Write three words that begin with *tr*.

7 _____ 8 _____ 9 _____

Write two sentences about your best friend.
Do not forget the capital letters and full stops!

10 _____

11 _____

Add *s* to each of these words to make it plural.

12 drink _____

13 flag _____

14 shop _____

15 goat _____

Now go to the Progress Chart to record your score!   Total   15

Paper 12

A mother dog gives birth to a litter of puppies.
Usually there are between six and ten puppies in a litter.
Puppies sleep for much of the time when they are first born.
To keep themselves warm they snuggle together.
They begin walking when they are about two weeks old.
Once they can walk they soon begin to explore and they begin to play at about three weeks old.
Once their adult teeth start to grow they spend much of their time chewing things!

Underline the right answers.

1 How many puppies does a mother dog usually have?

   (6–9 puppies, 5–9 puppies, 6–10 puppies)

2 At what age do the puppies begin to walk?

   (two days, two weeks, three weeks)

Answer these questions.

3 What is the word used to describe a group of puppies?

_____

4 Write a title for this piece of writing.

_____

Draw a line to link the words with the same spelling pattern.

5 sink   catch

6 dress   fist

7 mist   drink

8 match   mess

Choose the best word to fill the gap.

    run   ran   running

9 Josie _____ all the way home.

    packed   packing   putting

10 We _____ our clothes in the suitcase.

    his   their   her

11 Leela loved _____ riding lessons.

Copy these book titles.

Do not forget the capital letters!

12 junior dictionary

_____

13 a kangaroo's home

_____

14 learning to swim

_____

15 the journey

_____

Now go to the Progress Chart to record your score!   Total

Paper 13

When the wind blows

When the wind blows
Coats flap, scarves flutter.

When the wind blows
Branches groan, leaves mutter.

When the wind blows
Curtains swish, papers scatter.

When the wind blows
Gates creak, dustbins clatter.

When the wind blows
Doors slam, windows rattle.

When the wind blows...
Outside is a battle.

by John Foster

Underline the right answers.

1. How many times does **When the wind blows** appear in the poem?

   4   5   6

2. Which word in the poem rhymes with **flutter**?

   scatter   clatter   mutter

Answer these questions.

3. Find a word in the poem that rhymes with **rattle**. _____

4. Does the poem make you want to go outside in the wind? Why?

   _____

   _____

   _____

Underline the questions.

5–7 What is the time?

Here is your jumper.

Where is my PE kit?

Which book do you enjoy?

Hurry up or we will be late.

Make a word.

Add *st* to the beginning or end.

8 ____ep____

9 ____ing____

10 ____du____

Re-order the words to make a sentence.

11 wear? What I shall

_____

12 painted picture. a Dean beautiful

_____

Write the word.

13 walk + ed = _____

14 help + ed = _____

15 call + ed = _____

Total 15

Paper 14

Body parts

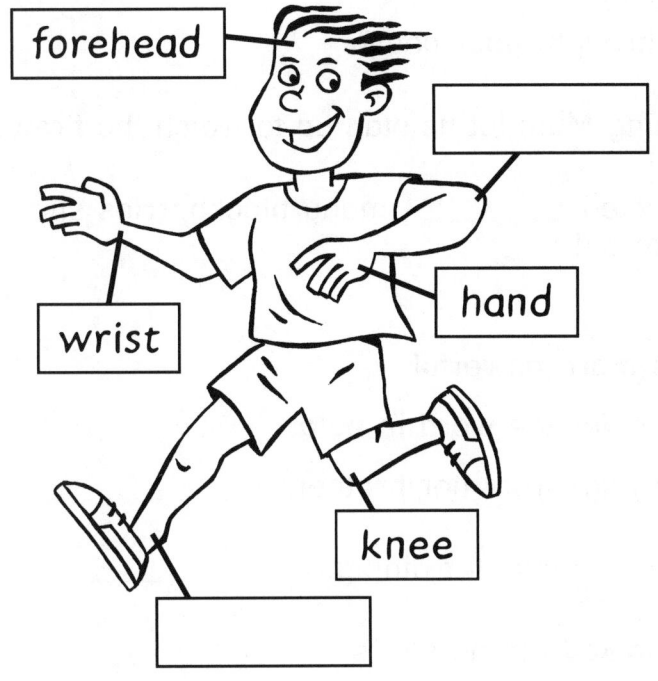

1–2 Fill in the two blank labels.

elbow   ankle

3–4 Add two more of your own labels to the body.

Add *fl* or *sl* to these letters to make a word.

5 _____ock

6 _____ame

7 _____ug

8 _____at

9 _____ot

2

2

5

Add a word from the box to each sentence.

Do not forget the capital letters!

| have | so | one |

10 _____ you brought your coat?

11 _____ evening Mum let us stay up to watch the fireworks.

12 Meena has collected _____ many blackberries she cannot hold them all!

Make these sentences more powerful.

Choose a different word for the word in **bold**.

13 Tia **took** the ball back from her brother. _____

14 Tim **enjoys** going to football training. _____

15 The angry girl **walked** up the stairs. _____

Now go to the Progress Chart to record your score! Total 15

Paper 15

Incy, Wincy Spider

Incy, wincy spider
Climbing up the spout
Down came the rain
And washed the spider out.

Out came the sun
And dried up all the rain,
So incy, wincy spider
Climbed up the spout again.

Anon

I Hear Thunder

I hear thunder,
I hear thunder,
Oh! don't you?
Oh! don't you?
Pitter, patter raindrops.
Pitter, patter raindrops.
I'm wet through.
I'm wet through.

I see blue skies.
I see blue skies.
Way up high.
Way up high.
Hurry up the sunshine.
Hurry up the sunshine.
I'll soon dry.
I'll soon dry.

Anon

Underline the right answer.

1 Which rhyme repeats each line?

(Incy, Wincy Spider; I Hear Thunder)

Answer these questions.

2 In the first poem, Incy, Wincy Spider does not give up.

How do we know this?

3 Find a word in the second poem that rhymes with **high**.

_____

4 Both rhymes are about the same thing.

What are they both about? _____

Underline the vowel letters.

5–7   h   i   g   d   a   u   b   t

Each sentence has a word that does not make sense.
Underline the wrong word. Write the correct word.

8–9 Daniel is move to a new school. _____

10–11 The dog loved his morning walked. _____

Write two words beginning with *sp*.

12 _____

13 _____

Write each *sp* word in a sentence.

14 _____

15 _____

Now go to the Progress Chart to record your score!   Total   15

Paper 16

Class 1 visited a farm.
This is Sam's recount of the visit.

> ### My Farm Visit
>
> On Thursday I went to a farm to see the animals.
> We went on a coach. I sat next to Elliot and we waved at the cars.
> At last we got to the farm.
> First we saw the cows. It was noisy and smelly but we saw the cows being milked. I was allowed to squeeze some milk from a cow's teat.
> We then went to feed the lambs with bottles of milk. The lambs loved the milk. Then they ran and jumped all over the place. One lamb nearly knocked me over!
> Then it was time for our packed lunch.
> After lunch we had time to throw food for the chickens. They looked really hungry.
> Then we all got back on the coach. This time I sat next to Eva. We felt very tired.
> It was a great visit to the farm. I want to go back again!
>
> by Sam Birdlip

Underline the right answers.

1. What day did the class visit the farm?

   (Monday, Wednesday, Thursday)

2. How many different creatures did Sam see?

   (2, 3, 4)

Answer these questions.

3 What did Class 1 do when they first arrived at the farm?
_____

4 Why did the lambs run and jump about?
_____

5 How do we know that Sam enjoyed the trip to the farm?
_____
_____

Underline the words with a sound that is similar to *ea* in m*ea*t.

6 sheet   seat   set

7 seal   step   sleep

Add a word in the gap to finish the sentence.

8 Gaby loved _____ with her dad.

9 Every morning Thomas _____ his face.

10 The rain _____ us on the way home.

Spell these words correctly.

11   skool ✗   _____

12   hous ✗   _____

13 larff ✗ _____

Write these sentences correctly.
Some capital letters are missing.

14 i always forget to hand my dinner money in.

_____

_____

15 Today i have to remember my homework.

_____

_____

Paper 17

Full of the Moon

It's full of the moon
The dogs dance out
Through brush and bush and bramble.
They howl and yowl
And growl and prowl.
They amble ramble scramble…
                                by Karla Kuskin

Roger the dog

Asleep he wheezes at his ease.
He only wakes to scratch his fleas.

He hogs the fire, he bakes his head
As if it were a loaf of bread.

He's just a sack of snoring dog.
You can lug him like a log.

You can roll him with your foot,
He'll stay snoring where he's put…
                                by Ted Hughes

Underline the right answers.

1 What are both these poems about?

   (the moon, dogs)

2 Which poem is set outside?

   (Full of the Moon, Roger the dog)

3 Find two words in the second poem that rhyme.

   _____   _____

4 Do you think Roger is an old dog or a puppy? Why?

   _____

   _____

Write two sentences about a dog.

It could be a dog you know or a dog you have seen. Be sure to use a full stop in each sentence.

5 _____

6 _____

Finish these word sums.

7 call + ing = _____

8 walk + ing = _____

9 lift + ing = _____

Circle the words with a sound that is similar to *ai* in t*ai*l.

10–13

snail	coat	spoon	sand
kind	tale	hay	
cape	hat	munch	kite

Copy and add the missing capital letters.

14 queen elizabeth _____

15 sir gareth bigears _____

Now go to the Progress Chart to record your score!   Total   15

Paper 18

Sometimes charts are a good way of recording information.

Weather record

Day	Weather
Monday	cloudy
Tuesday	windy
Wednesday	rainy
Thursday	rainy
Friday	
Saturday	rainy
Sunday	sunny

Answer these questions.

1 Look at the weather symbol for Friday. Write in the missing word on the chart.

2 What was the weather like on Tuesday? _____

3 How many days was it rainy? _____

4 Which day of the week was the best day to play outside?

_____

Use these letters to make four words that rhyme.

Add the letters to the gaps.

      p   k   m   h   s

5–8 ___y   ___igh   ___ie   ___ ___y

Write two questions.

Remember to add the question marks.

9 _____

10 _____

Write two words that might fit in the gap in this sentence.

Ravi _____ to Helen's house.

11 _____

12 _____

Circle the consonant letters.

13–15 e   r   u   i   k   v   a   o

Now go to the Progress Chart to record your score!   Total   15

Paper 19

This is Jessica's recount of a Creativity Day held at her school.

> On Friday, Crudwell Primary School had a Creativity Day. First Class 2 did some Aboriginal paintings. I did a snake and some beetles. I felt very happy when I had finished.
> Next, after playtime, we did some pottery. I made my snake from my Aboriginal painting.
> After lunch we did some more pottery but this time we did it out of a book. I did a chicken!
> Then we made some didgeridoos. I had one of the longest, it was really fun!
> We had time for a quick playtime and then it was home time.
>
> by Jessica Lindman

Underline the right answers.

1 What did Jessica paint on her Aboriginal painting?

   (a chicken, a snake, a snake and some beetles)

2 Do you think Jessica enjoyed the Creativity Day?

   (Yes, No)

Answer this question.

3 What do you think Jessica enjoyed making the most? How do you know?

_____

_____

These letters are muddled. Sort the letters to make a colour word.

   4 l e u b   _____

   5 k n p i   _____

   6 w r o b n   _____

Re-order the words to make a sentence.

   7 am I going What to the time party?

   _____

   8 cows grass the field. in The munch the

   _____

Underline the words with a similar sound to *oa* in b*oa*t.

9–12   frog   coat   nose   mat

       snow   tube   moon   bike

       tape   spider   doze

These headings can be found in a book called *My Body*.
Copy these headings. Remember to add the capital letters.

  13 what we eat

   _____

  14 inside our bodies

   _____

  15 what happens when we sleep?

   _____

Now go to the Progress Chart to record your score!   Total   15

Paper 20

The sun did not shine.
It was too wet to play.
So we sat in the house
All that cold, cold, wet day.
I sat there with Sally.
We sat there, we two.
And I said, "How I wish
We had something to do!"
Too wet to go out
And too cold to play ball.
So we sat in the house.
We did nothing at all.
So all we could do was to
Sit!
    Sit!
        Sit!
            Sit!
And we did not like it.
Not one little bit.
And then
Something went BUMP!
How that bump made us jump!
We looked!
Then we saw him step in on the mat!
We looked!
And we saw him!
The Cat in the Hat!
And he said to us,
"Why do you sit there like that?"
"I know it is wet
And the sun is not sunny.
But we can have
Lots of good fun that is funny!"

From *The Cat in the Hat* by Dr Seuss

Underline the right answer.

1. What was the weather like?

   (sunny, wet, windy)

Answer these questions.

   2 Find a word in the poem that rhymes with **cat**. _____

   3 What does the Cat in the Hat want the children to do?

   _____

Copy the book titles.
Remember the capital letters!

   4 the rat meets a cat

   _____

   5 a windy day

   _____

   6 what not to eat

   _____

Look at this picture. What does it make you think about?

Write two questions about the picture.

   7 _____

   8 _____

Write four words you would use if you were writing about a beach holiday. Here is an example: _paddle_

9 _____   10 _____

11 _____   12 _____

Write a word that has the same spelling pattern and rhymes with each of these words.

13 boy _____

14 new _____

15 soon _____

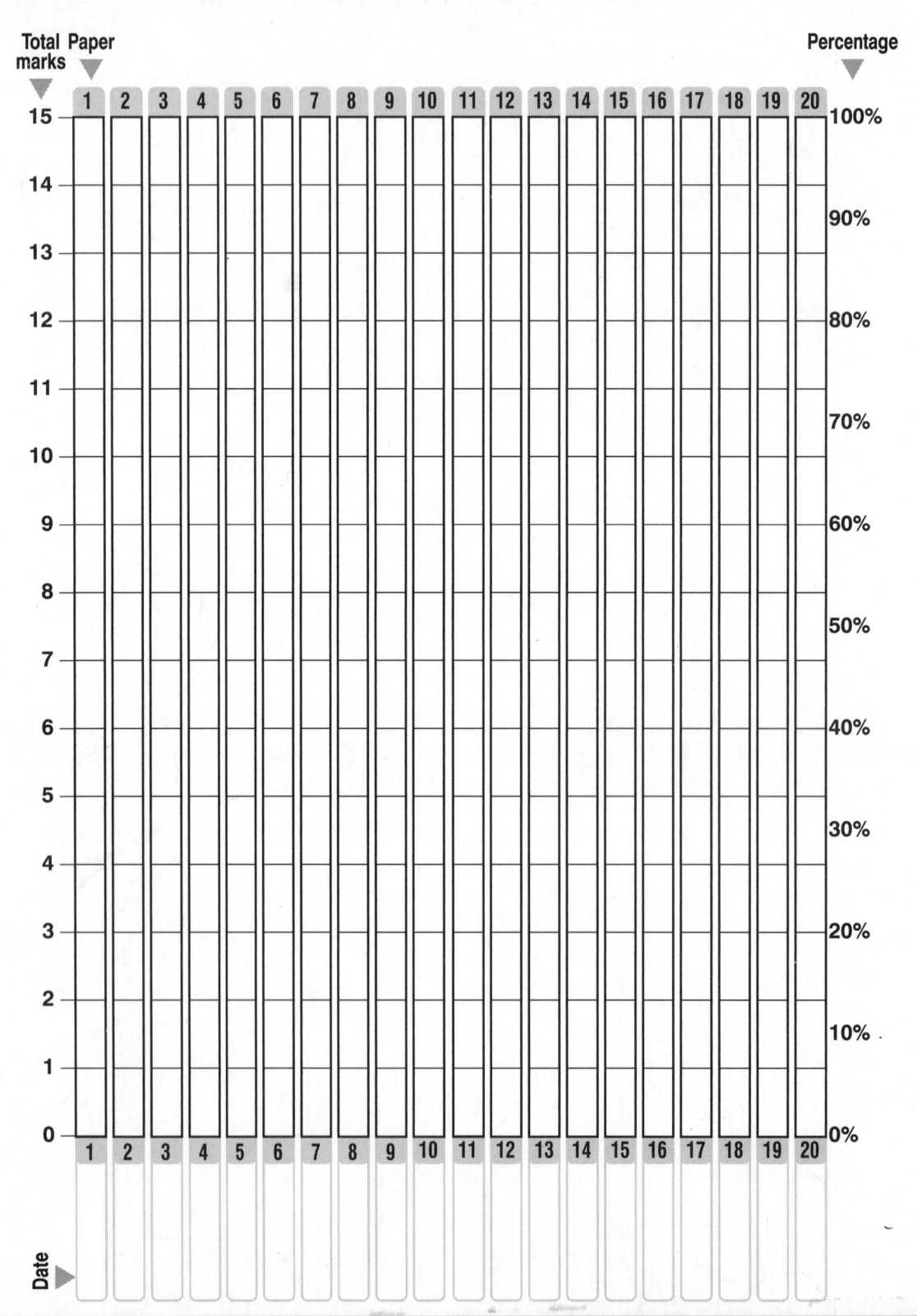

Progress Chart   English 5-6 years

Total marks	Paper																				Percentage
	1	2	3	4	5	6	7	8	9	10	11	12	13	14	15	16	17	18	19	20	
15																					100%
14																					
13																					90%
12																					80%
11																					
10																					70%
9																					60%
8																					
7																					50%
6																					40%
5																					
4																					30%
3																					20%
2																					
1																					10%
0																					0%
	1	2	3	4	5	6	7	8	9	10	11	12	13	14	15	16	17	18	19	20	

Date

When you've finished the book read the Next Steps →